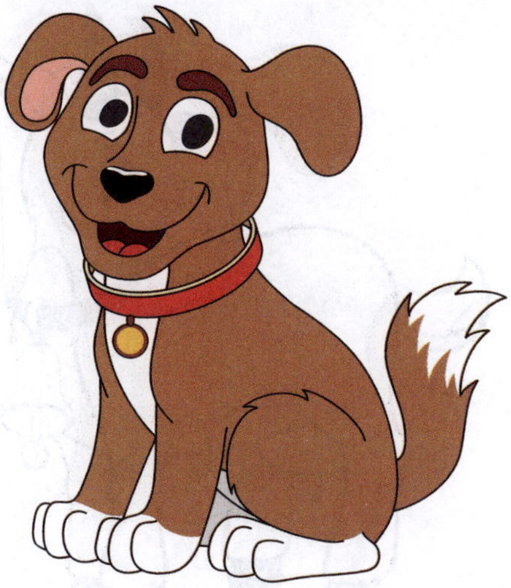

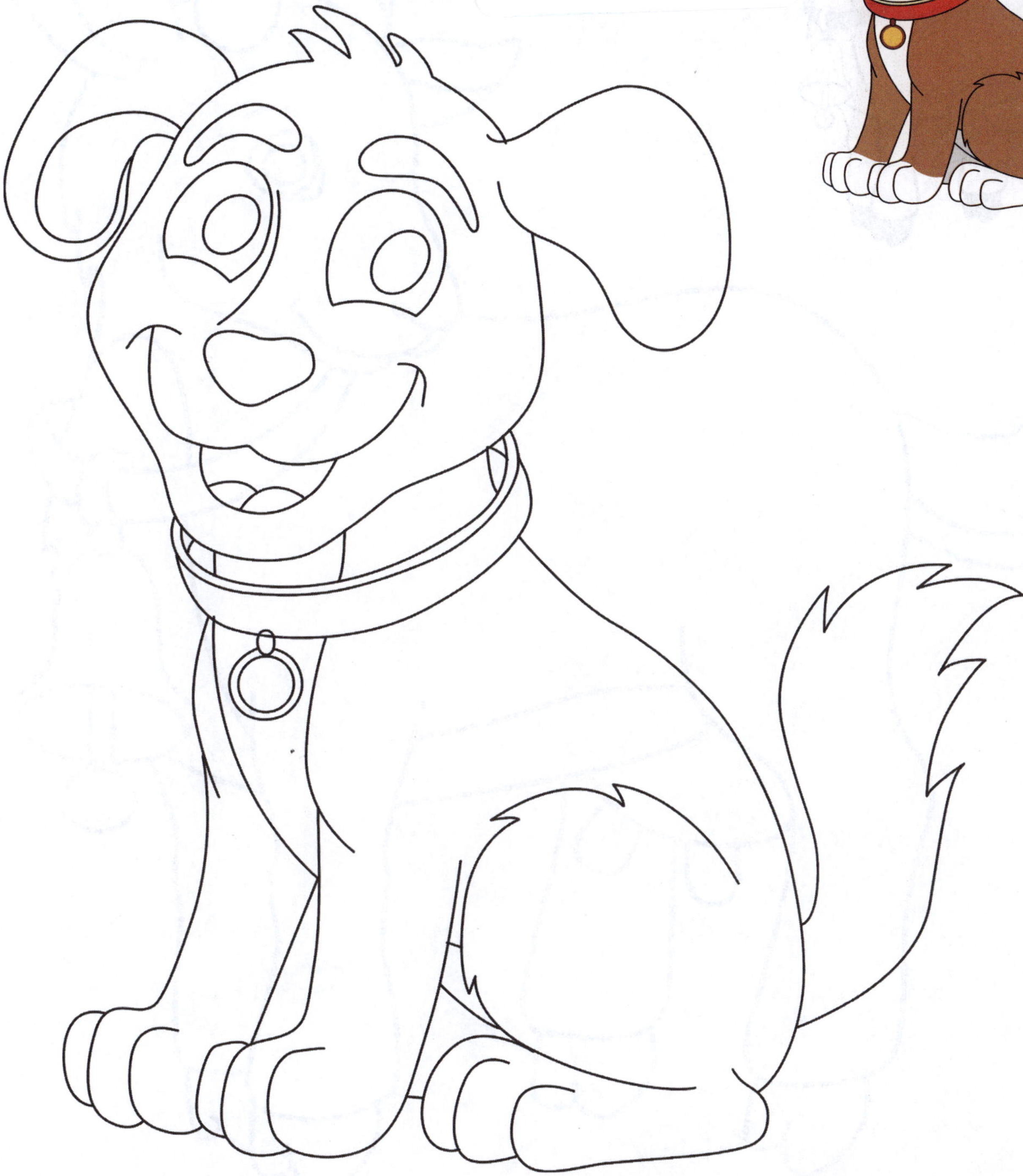

dog

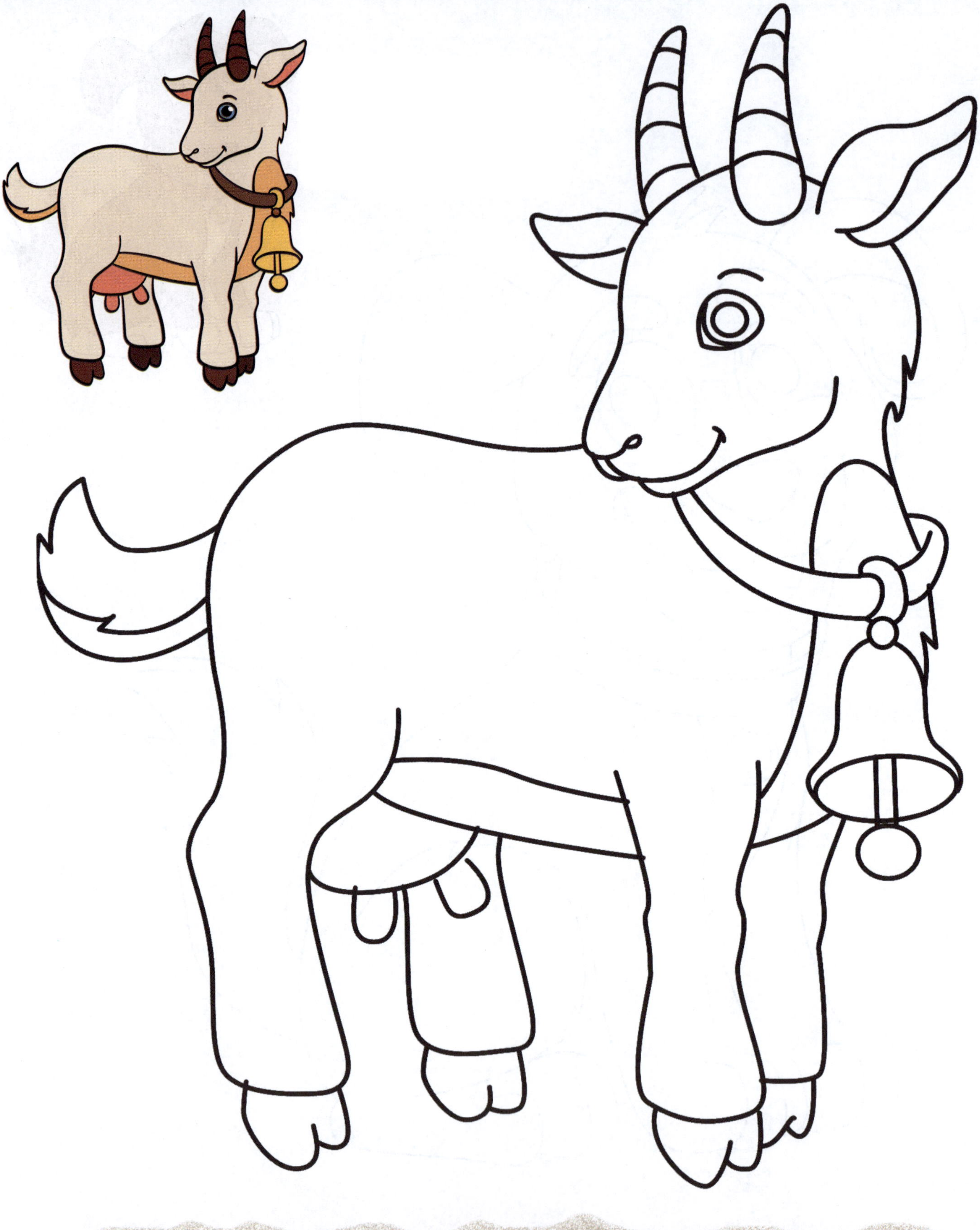

goat

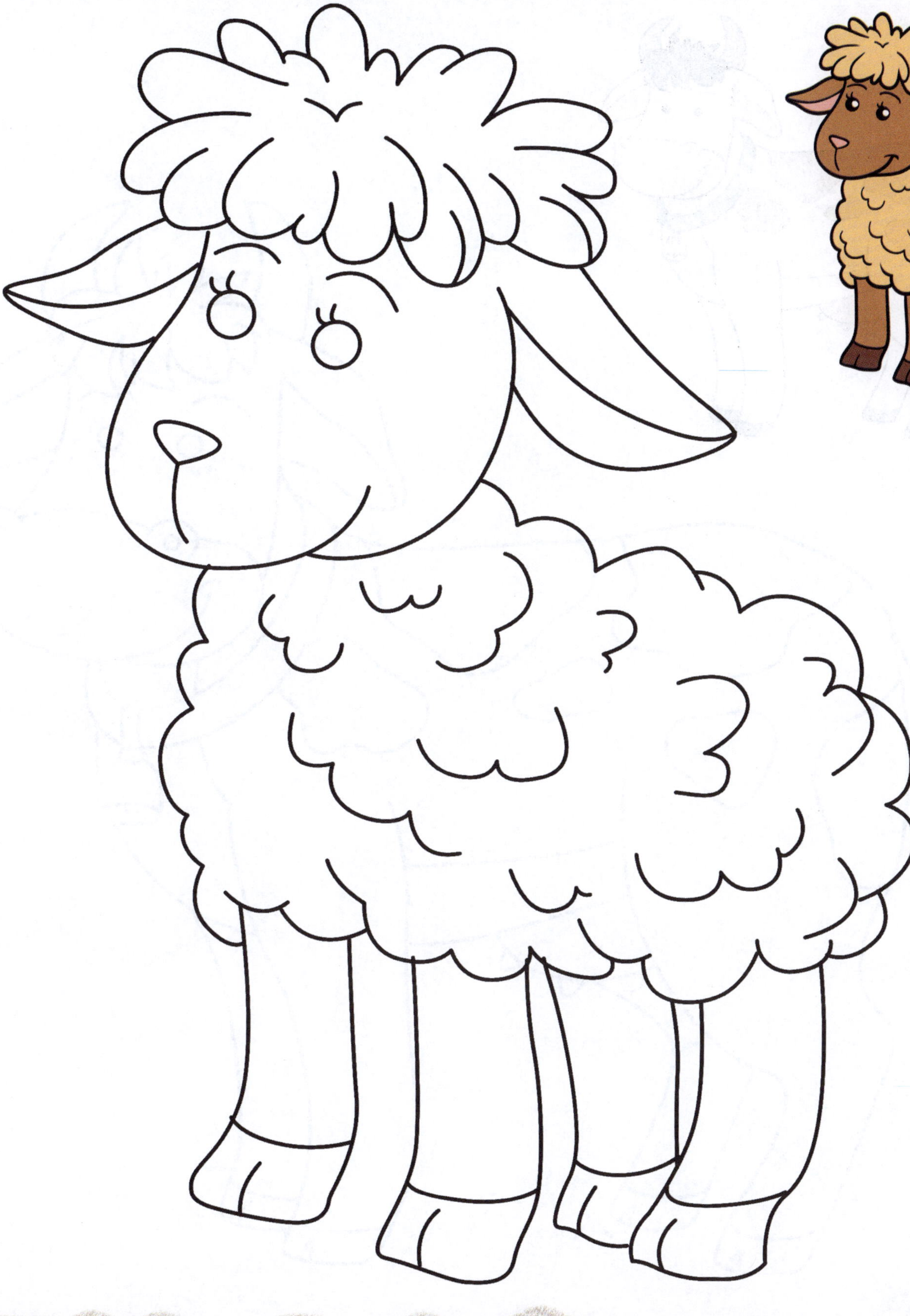

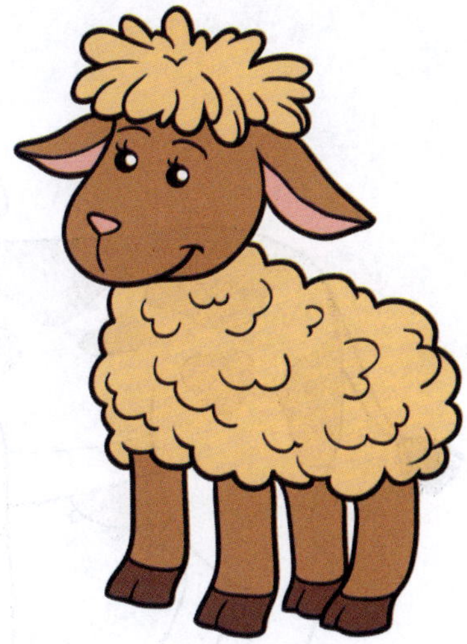

sheep

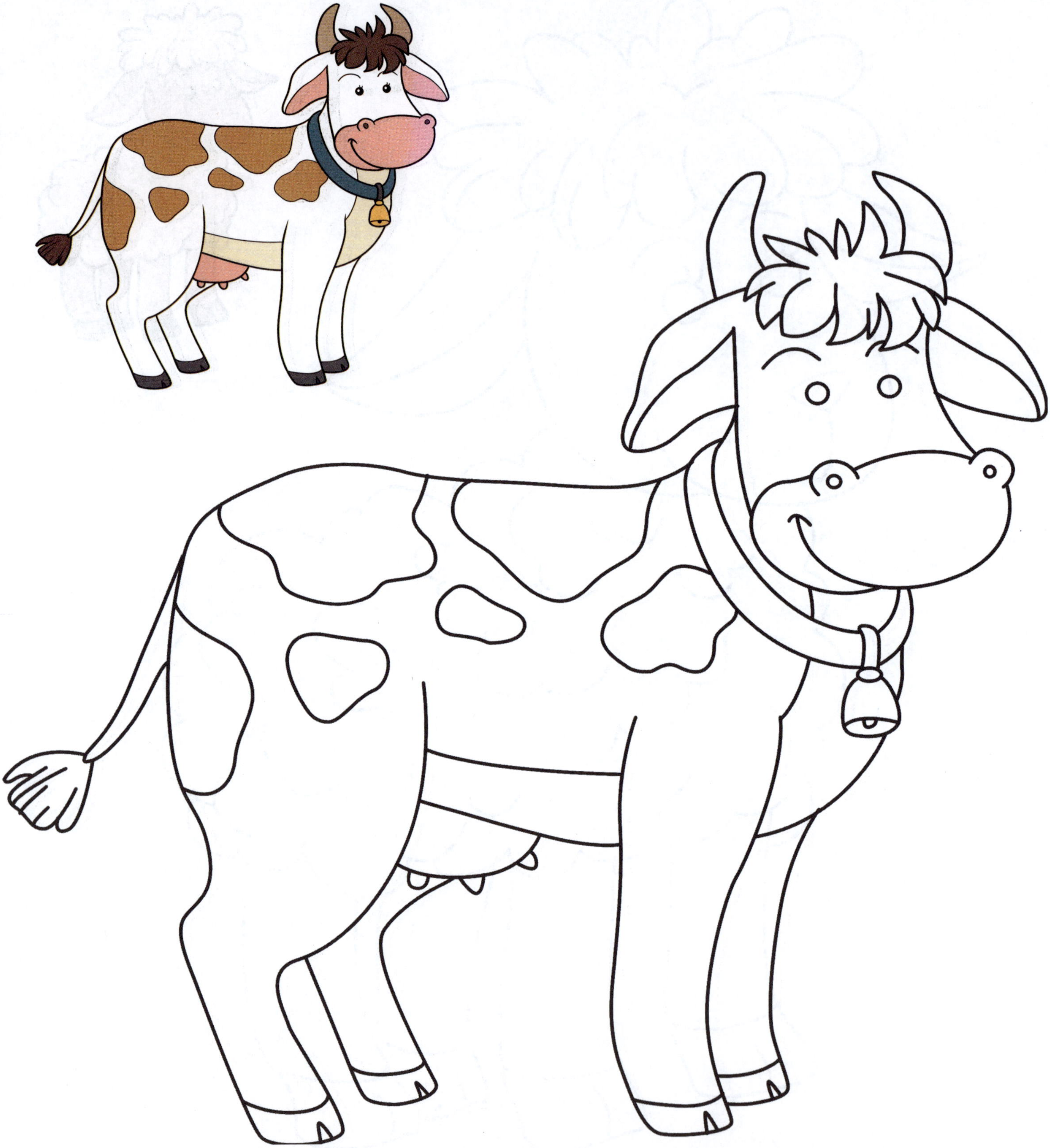

cow

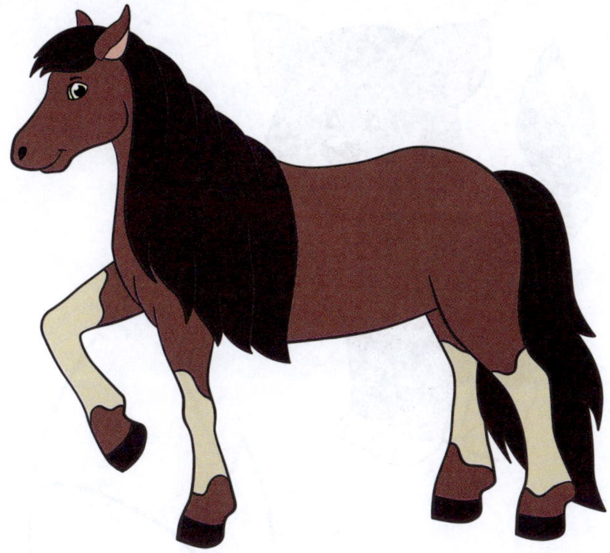

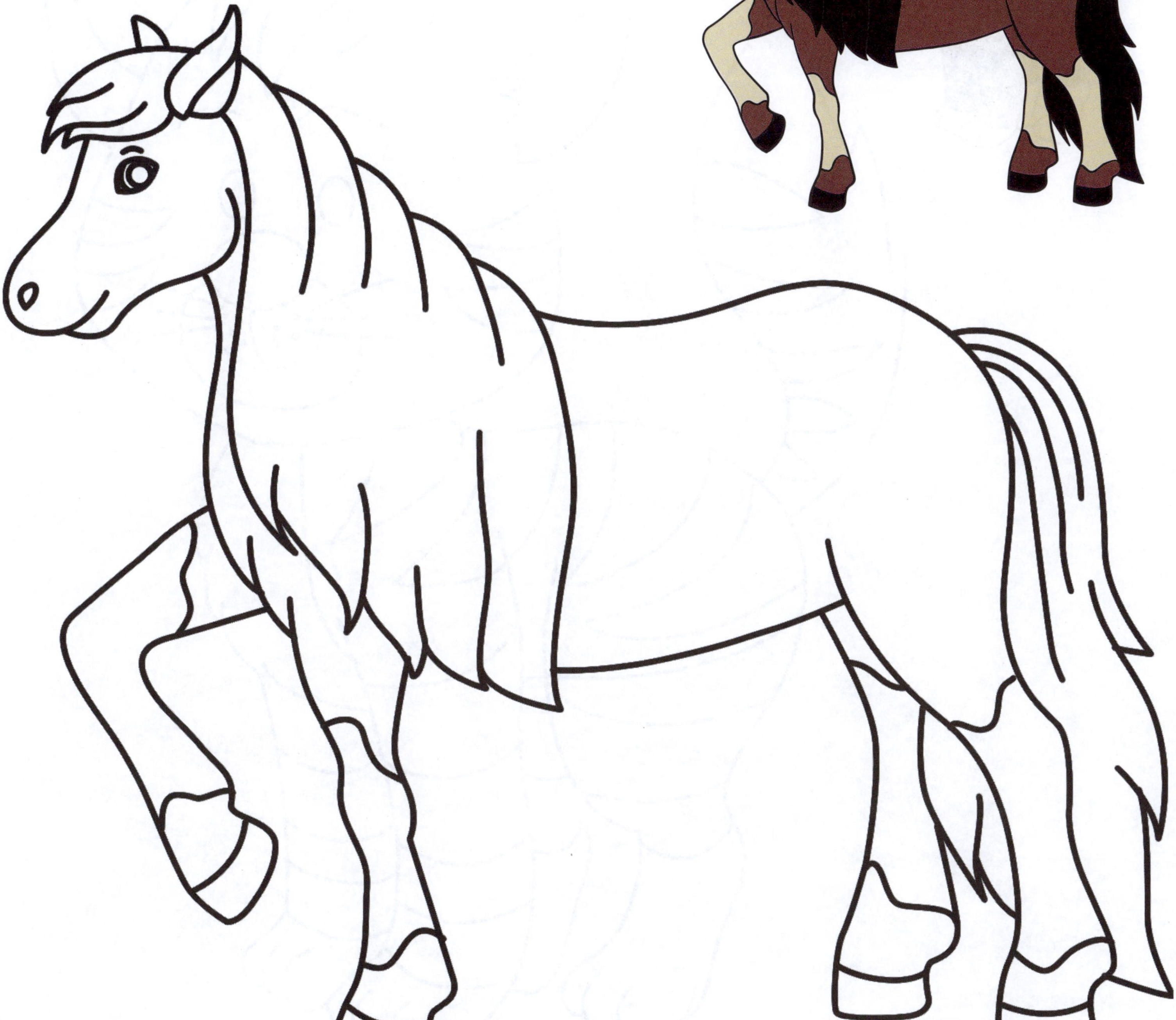

horse

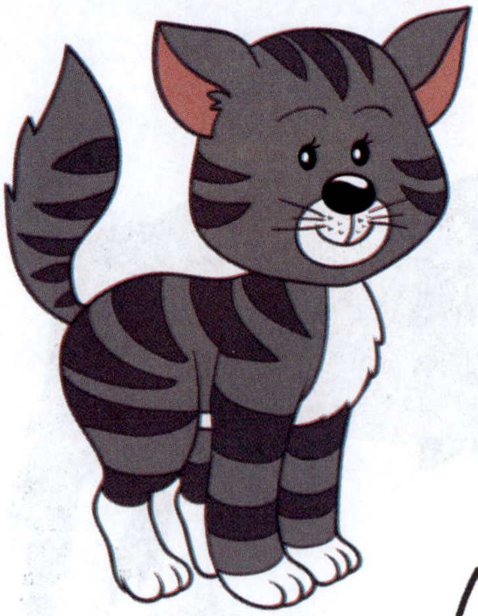

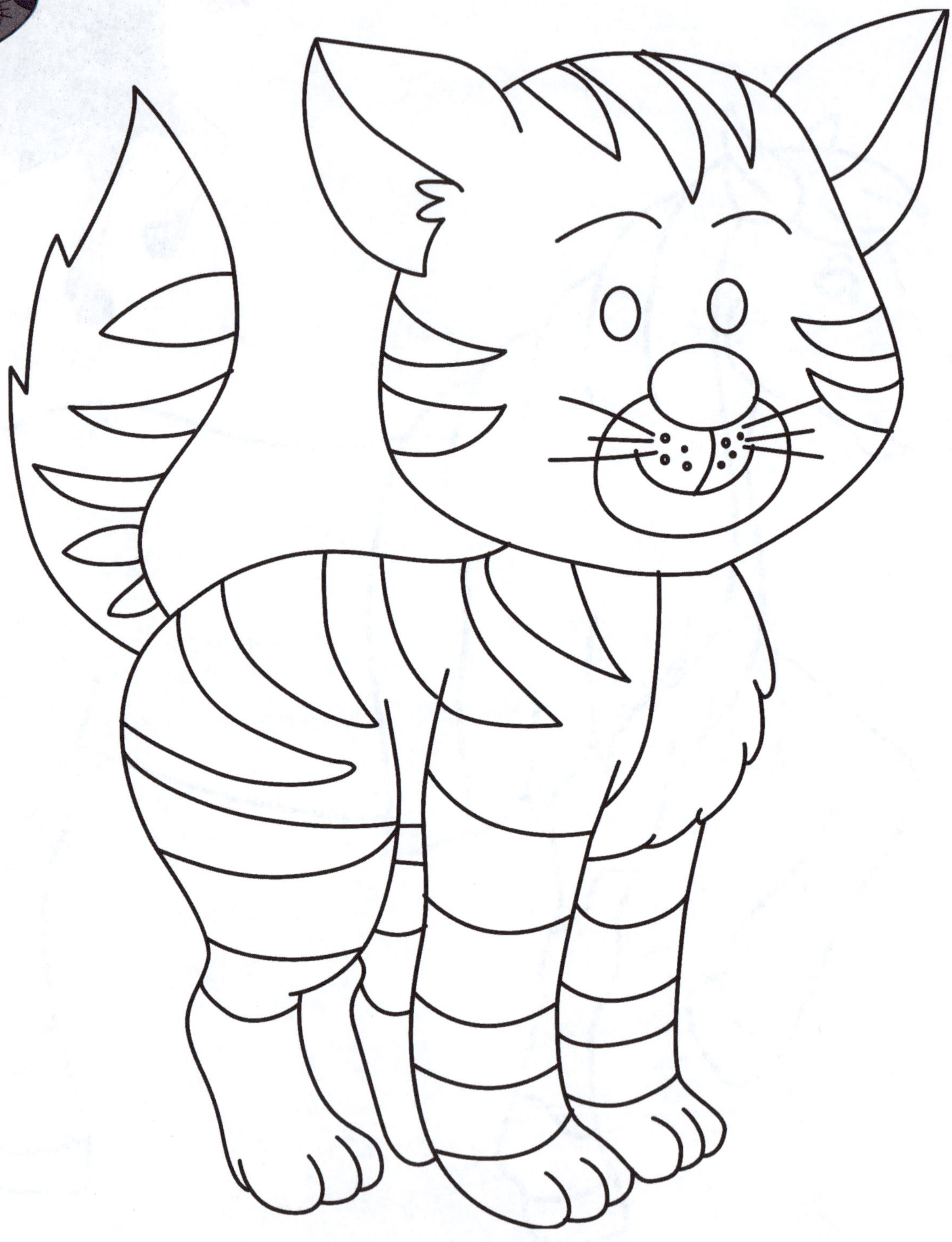

cat

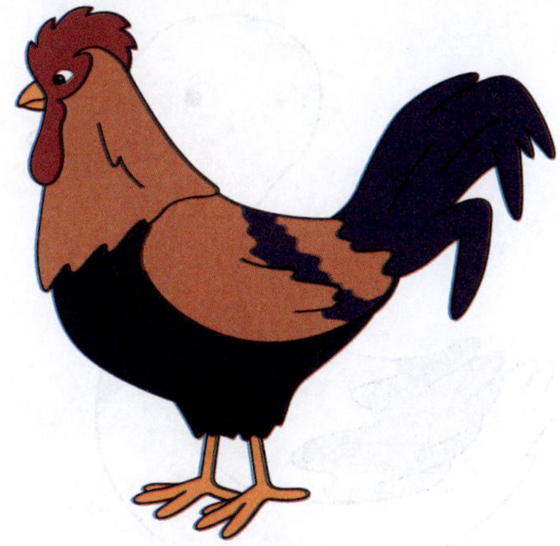

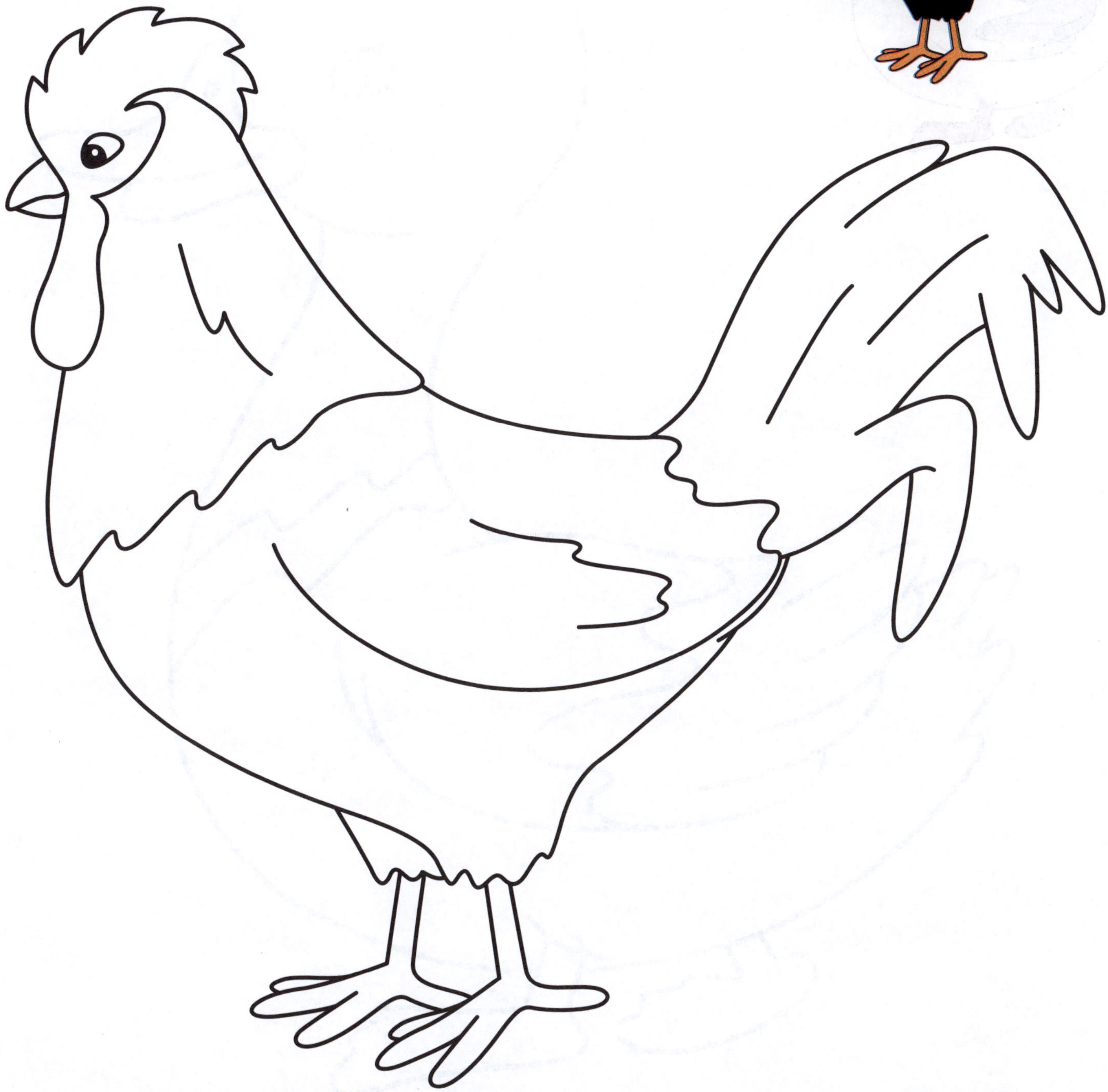

rooster

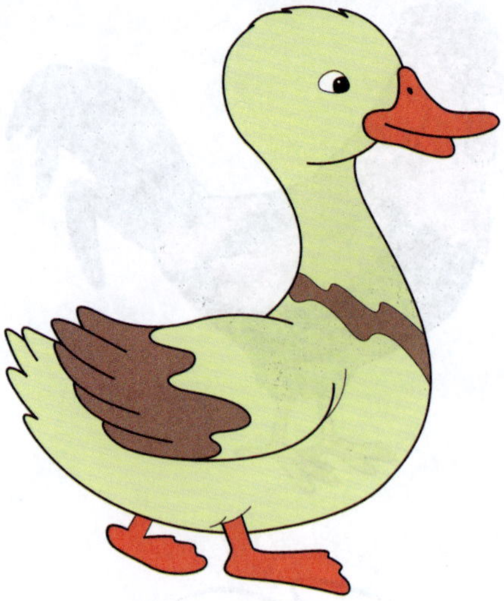

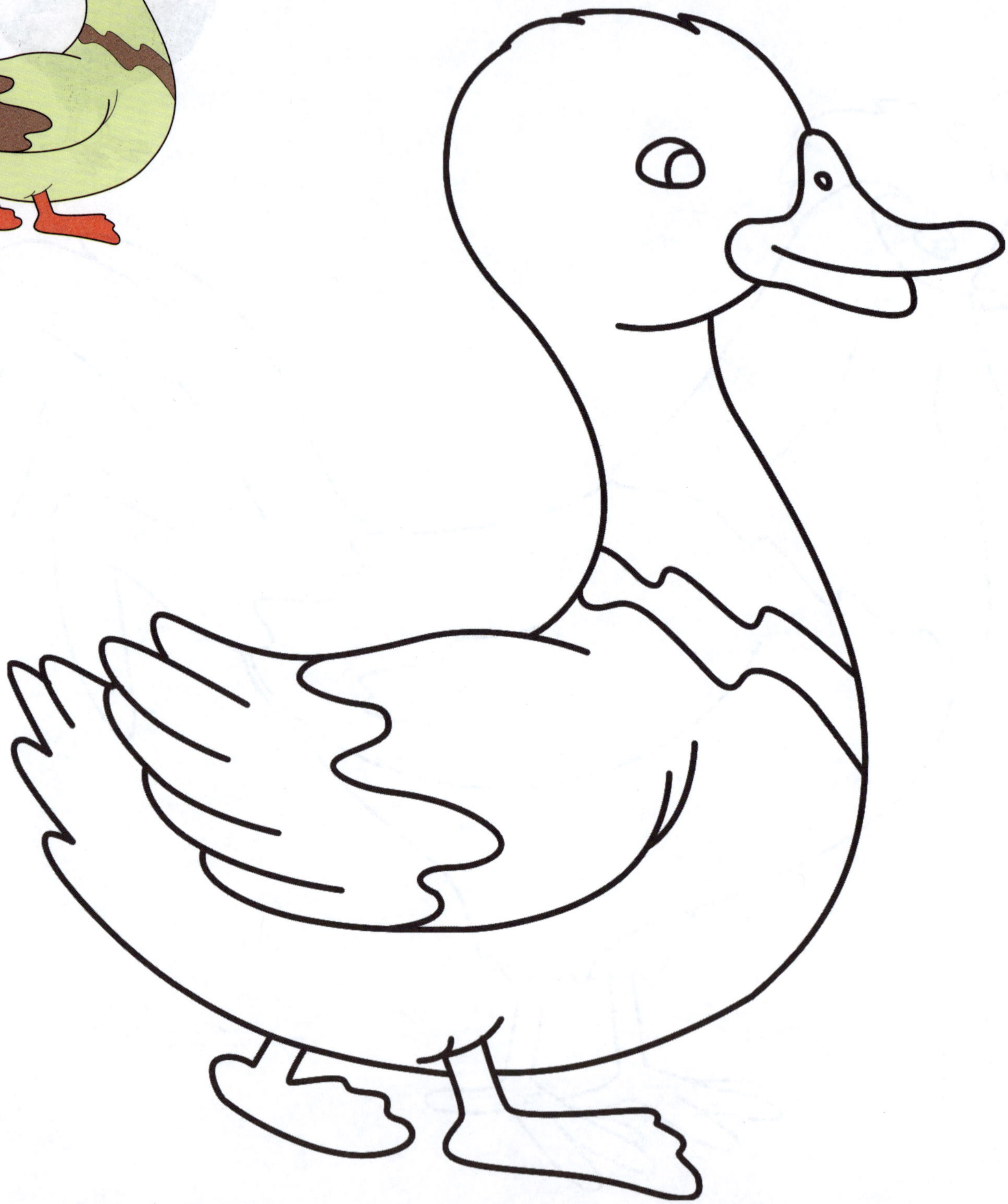

duck

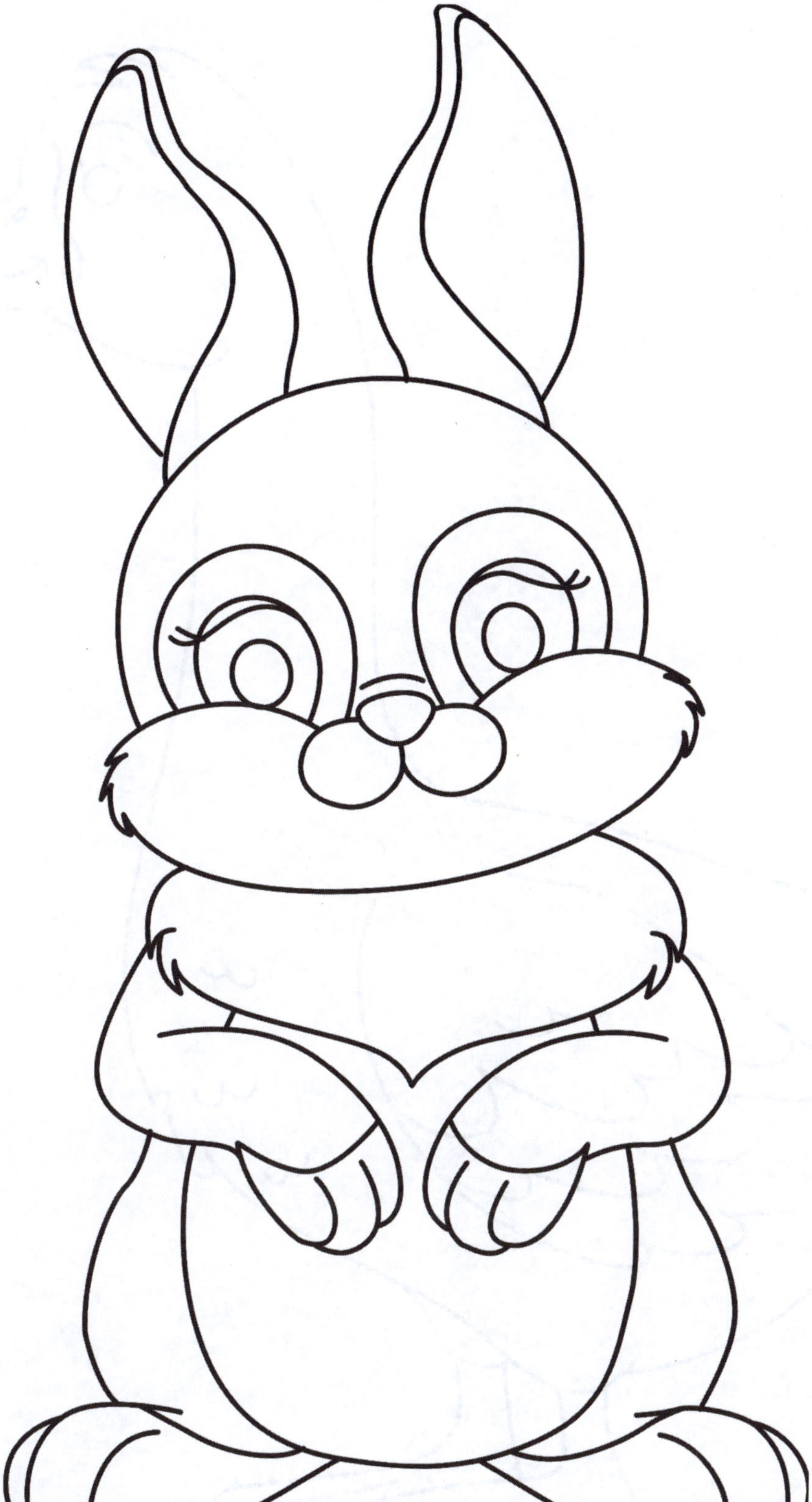

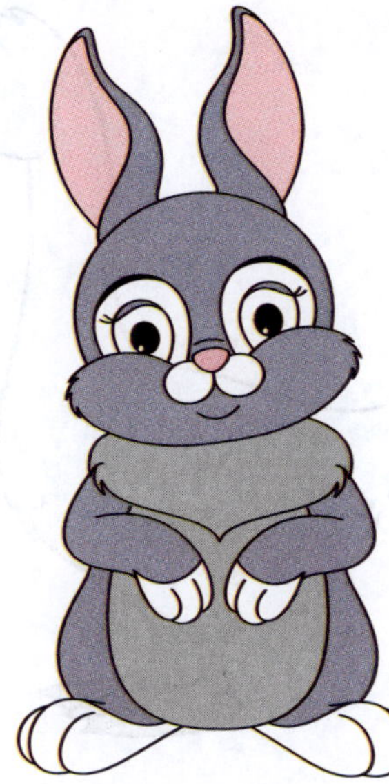

rabbit

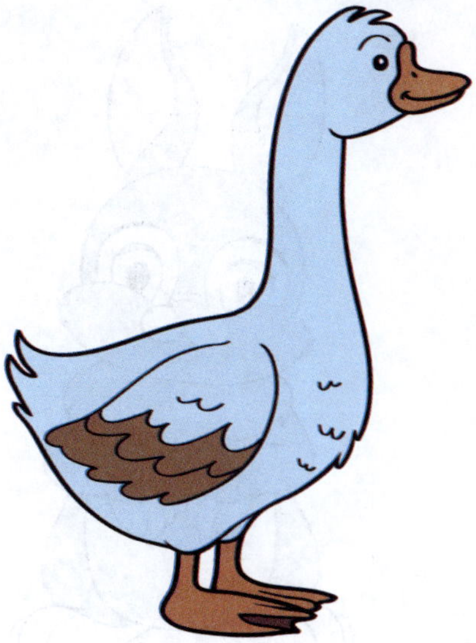

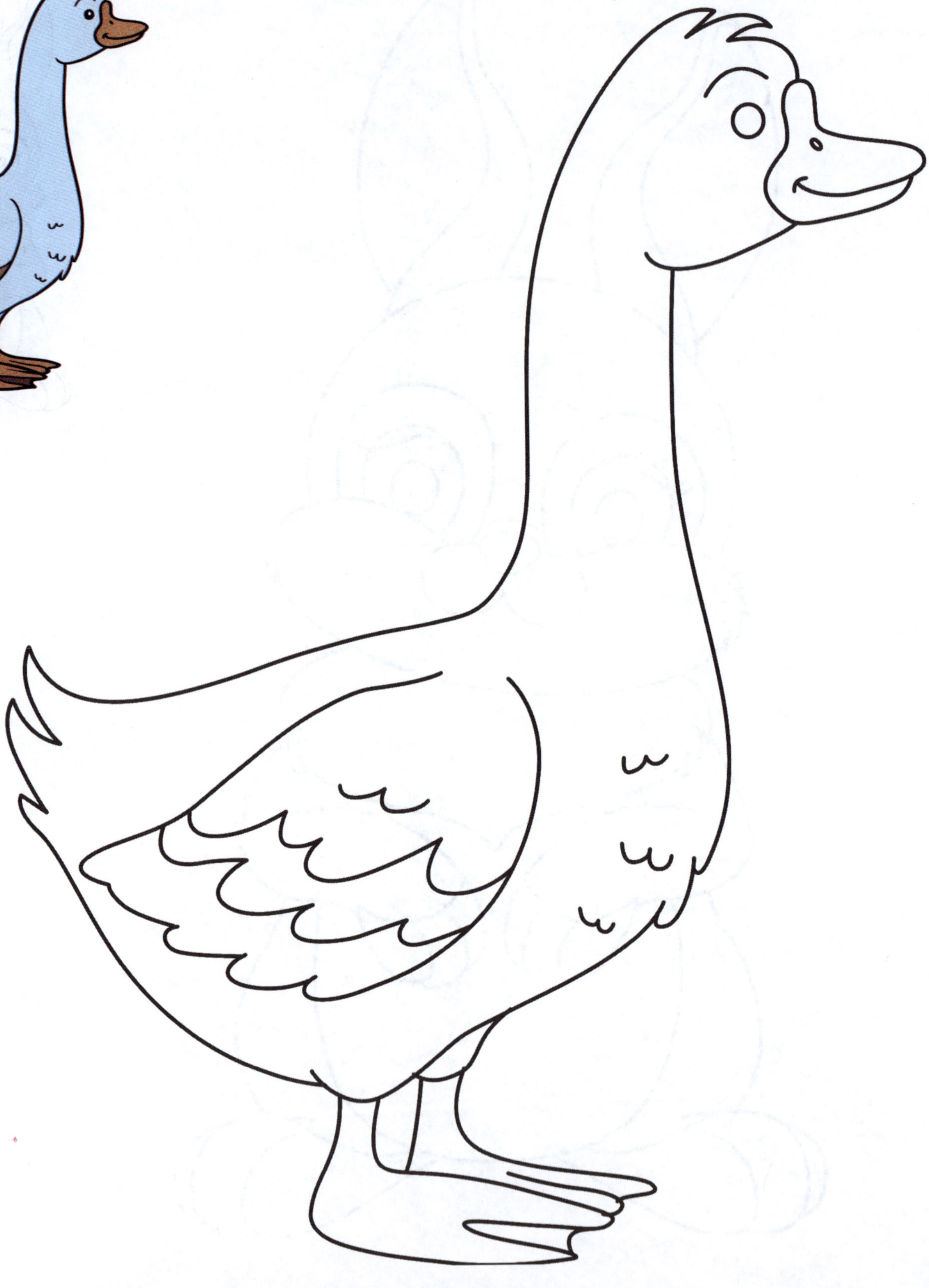

goose

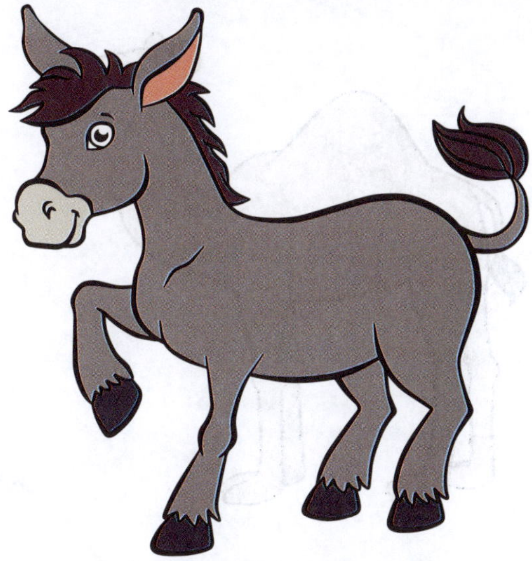

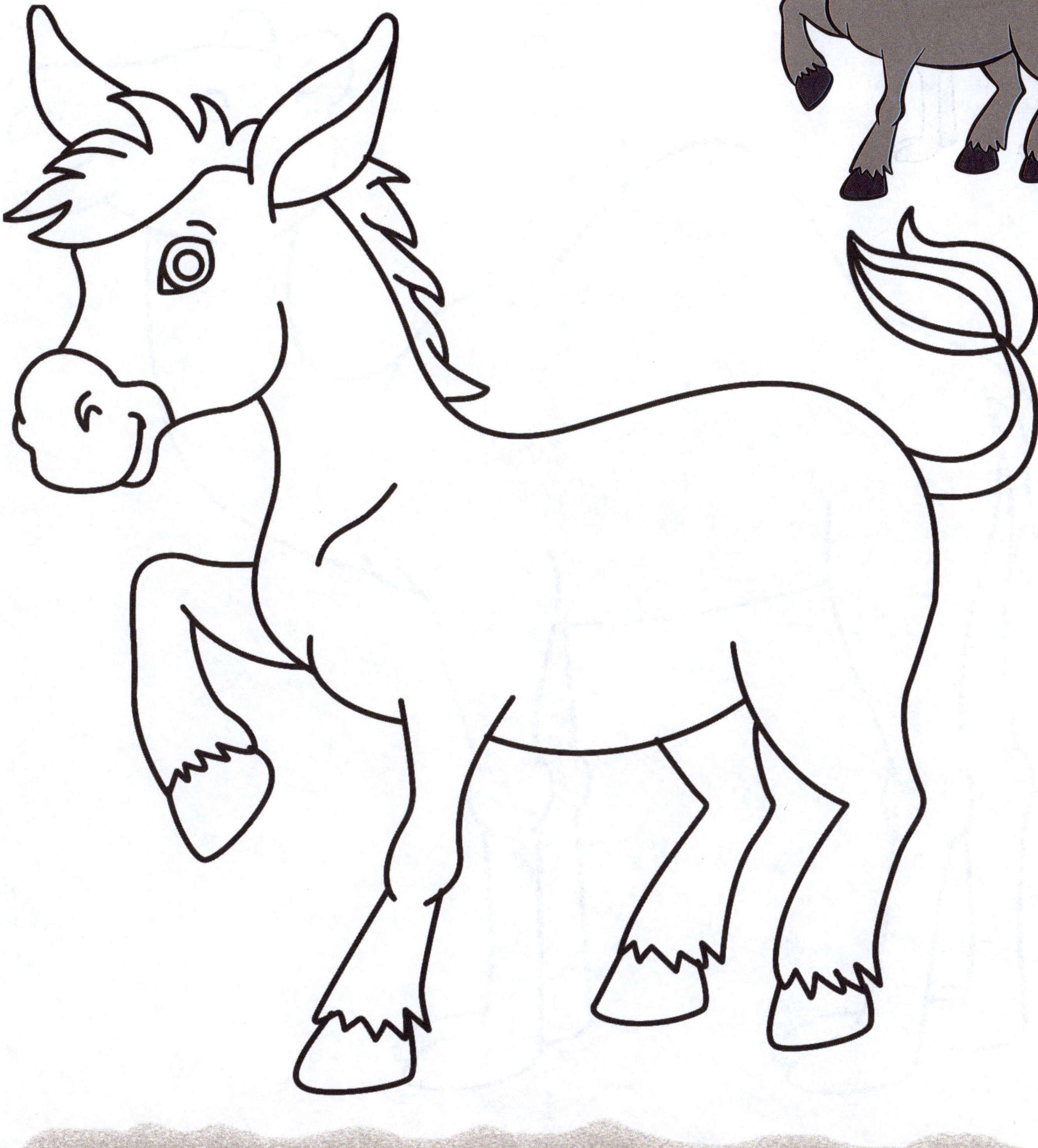

Donkey

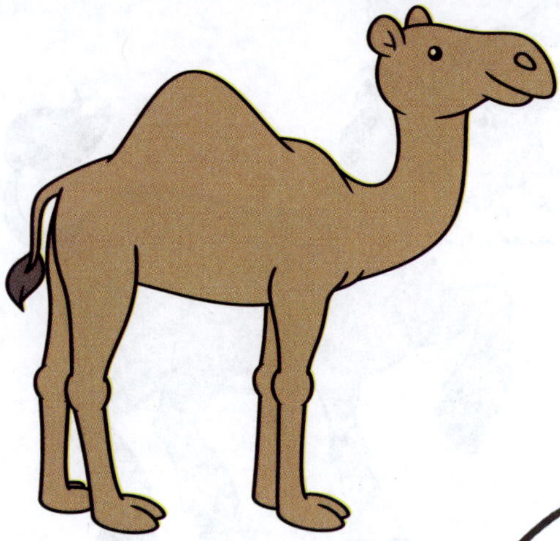

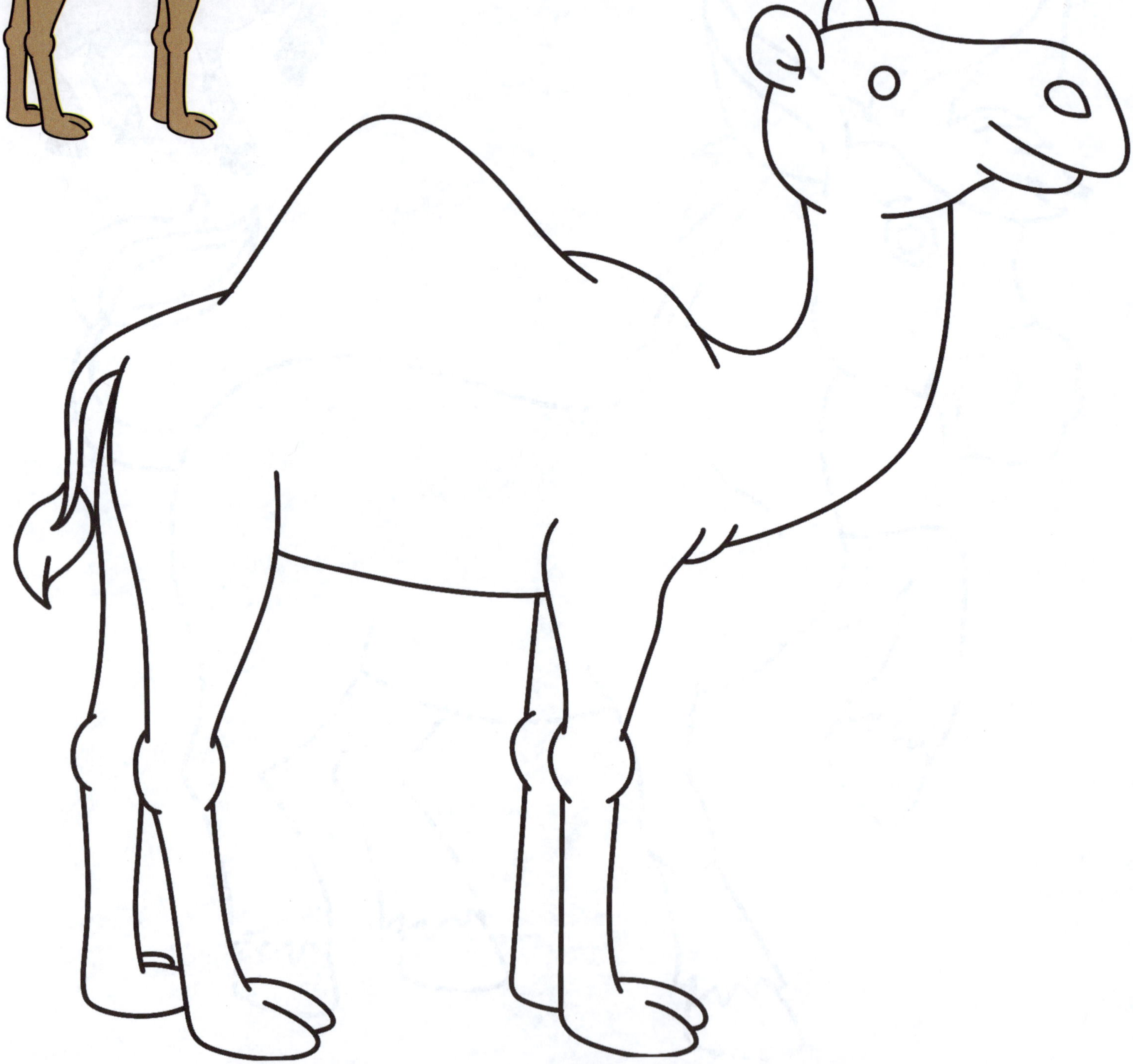

camel

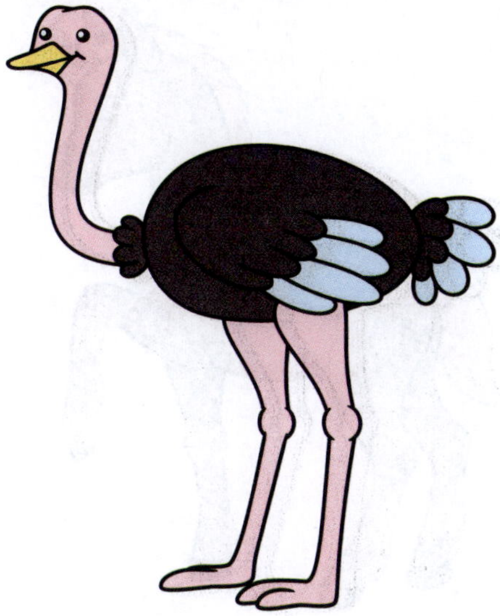

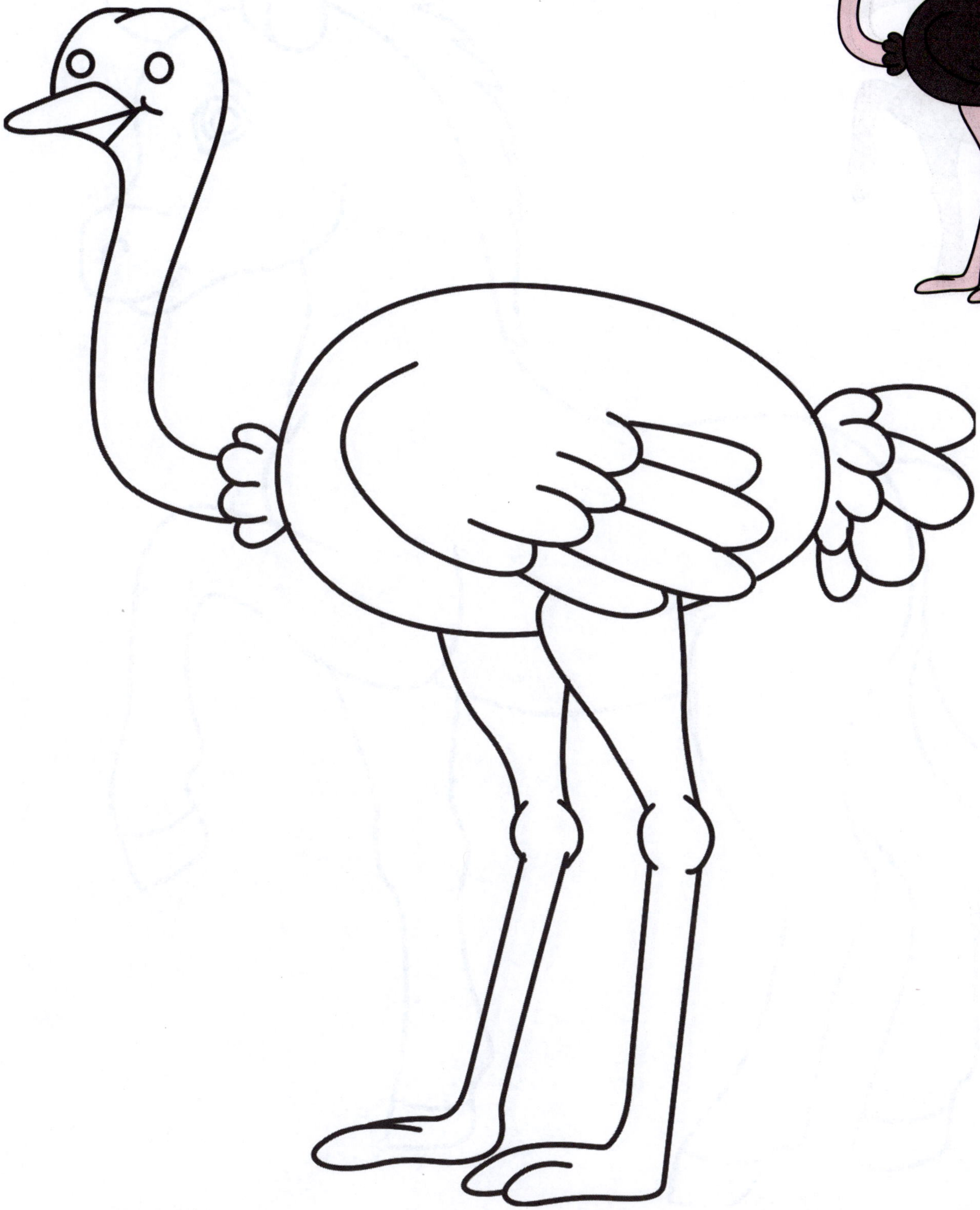

ostrich

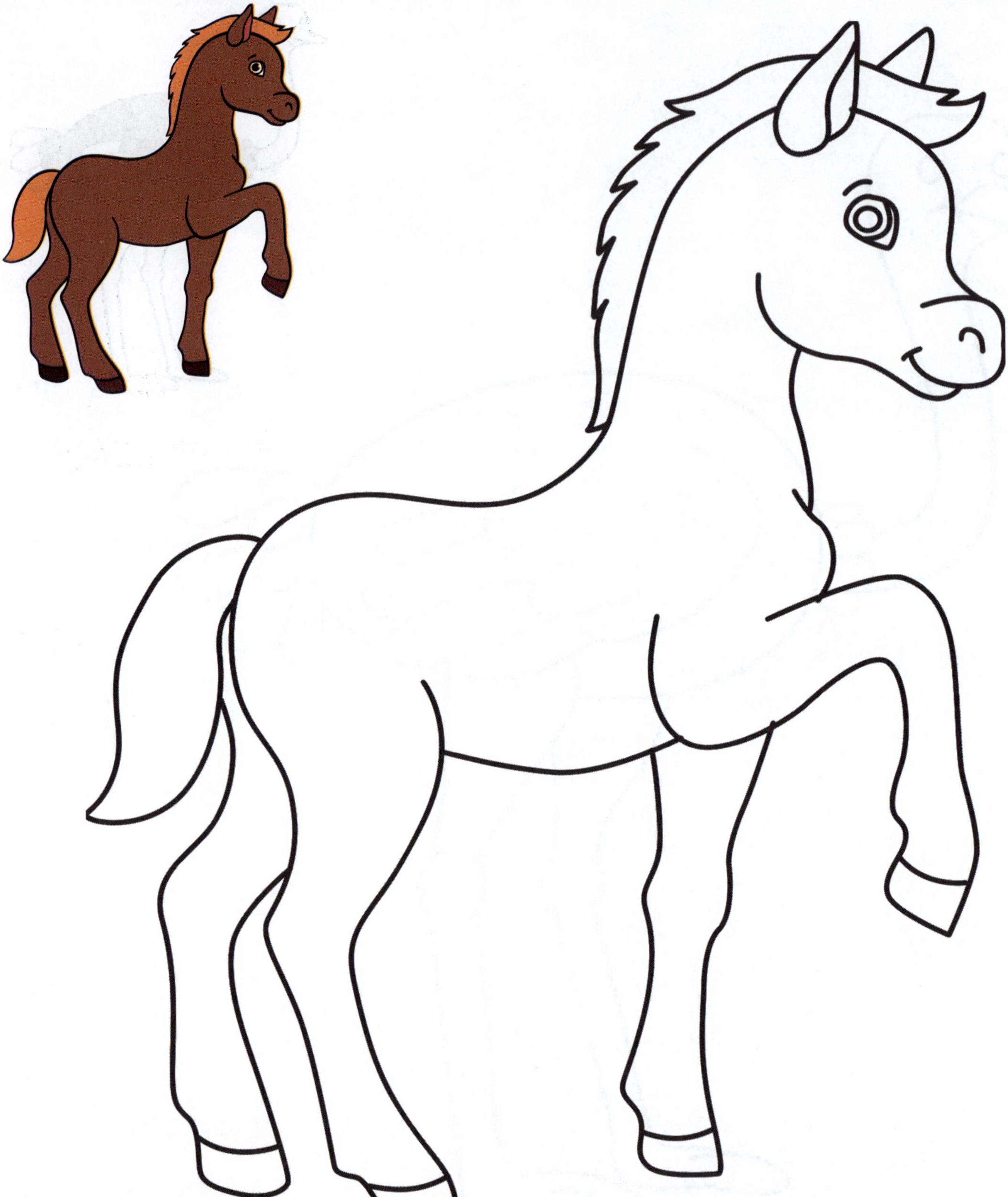

fowl

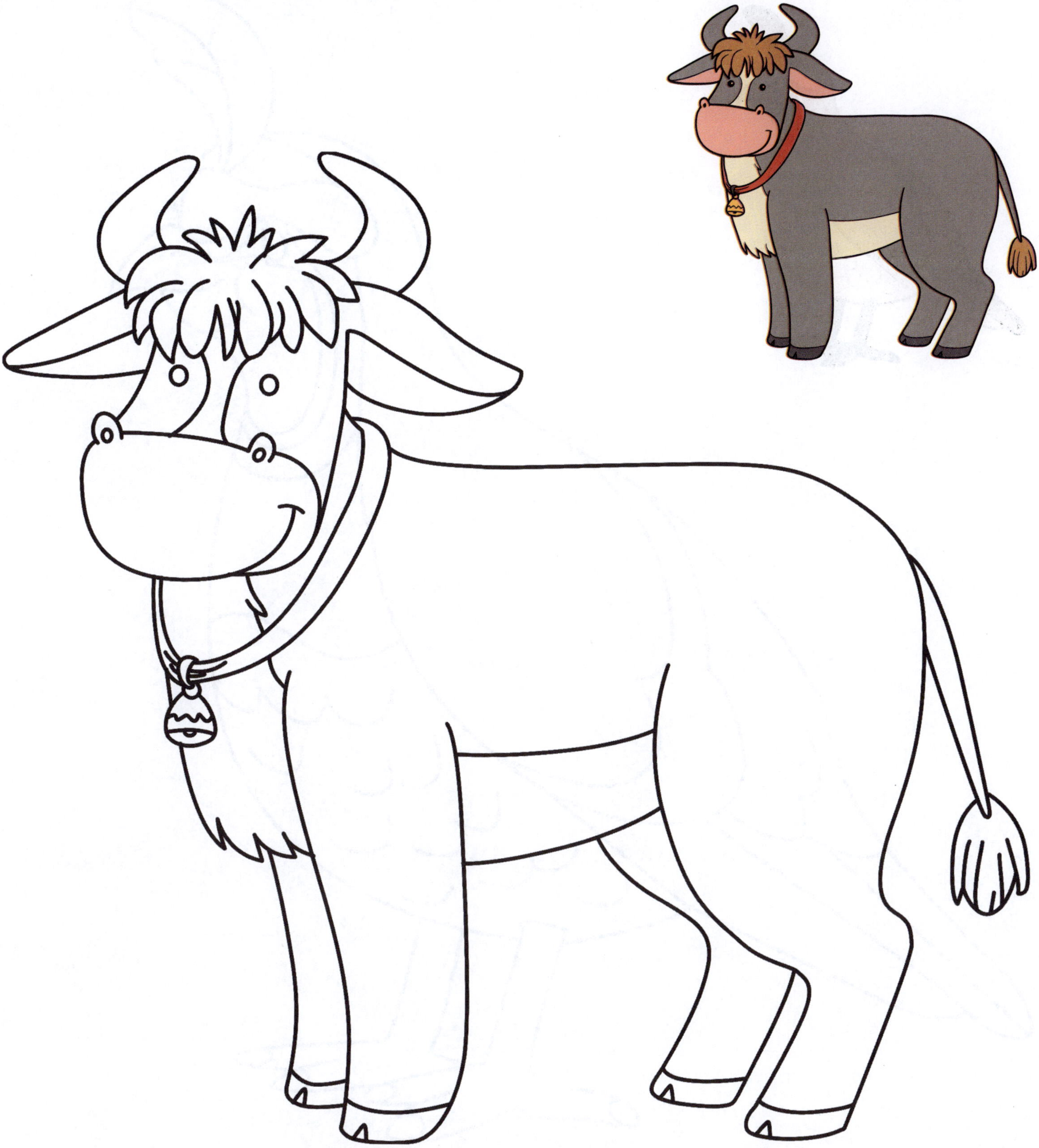

bull

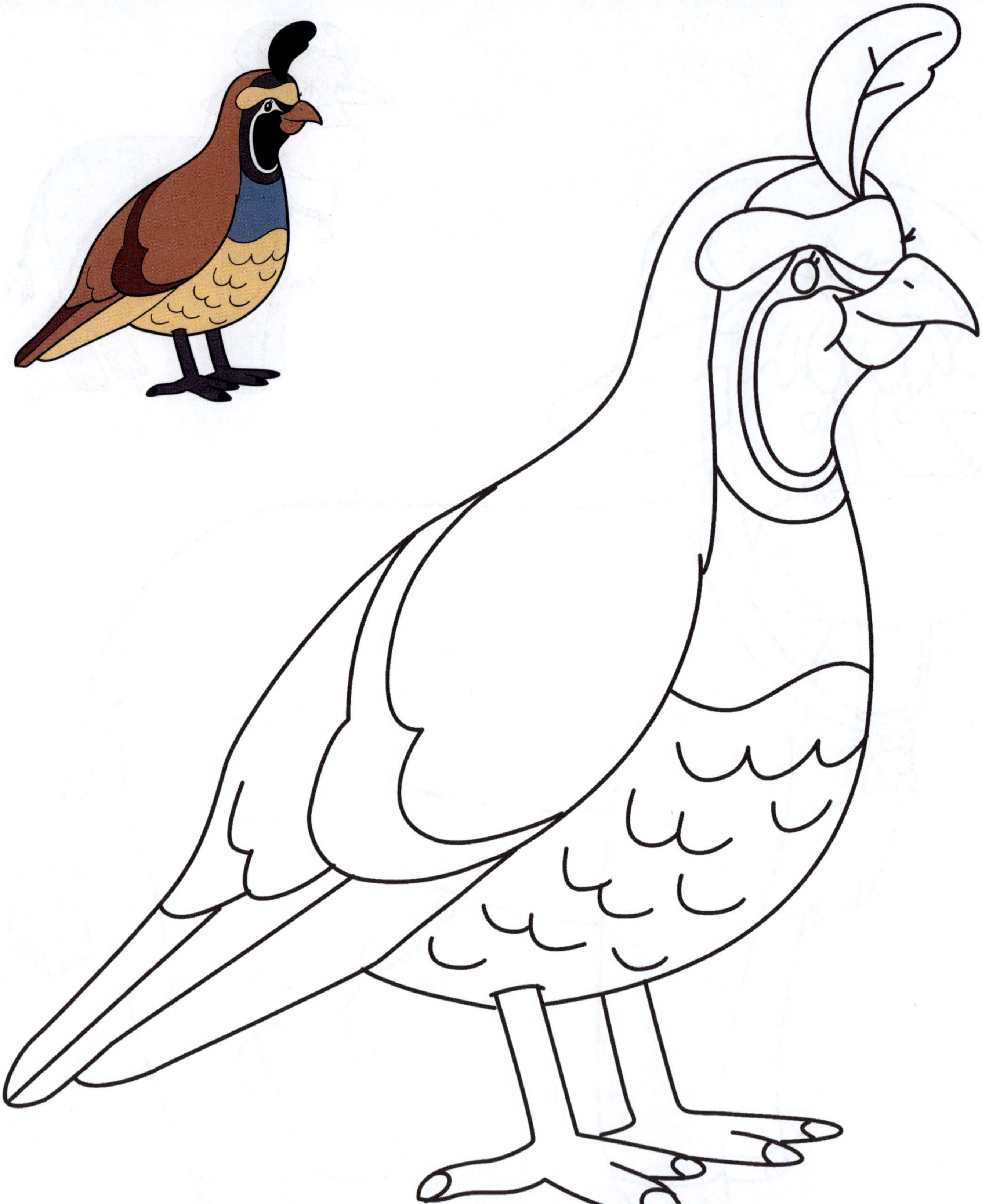

quail